I CAN FIX MY...

by
LILETTA HARLEM

Copyright © 2020 by Liletta Harlem
All rights reserved.

No part of this publication may be reproduced, stored in a retrieval system, or transmitted in any form or by any means, electronic, mechanical, scanning, recording, photocopying, or otherwise, without the prior written permission of the author.

Limit of Liability/Disclaimer of Warranty: This publication is designed to provide accurate and authoritative information in regard to the subject matter covered. It is sold with the understanding that neither the author nor the publisher is engaged in rendering legal, investment, accounting, or other professional services. While the publisher and author have used their best efforts in preparing this book, they make no representations or warranties with respect to the accuracy or completeness of the contents of this book and specifically disclaim any implied warranties of merchantability or fitness for a particular purpose. No warranty may be created or extended by sales representatives or written sales materials. The advice and strategies contained herein may not be suitable for your situation. You should consult with a professional when appropriate. Neither the publisher nor the author shall be liable for any loss of profit or any other commercial damages, including but not limited to special, incidental, consequential, personal, or other damages.

I Can Fix My…By Liletta Harlem

1.SEL023000 2.SEL016000 3.SEL042000
Paperback ISBN: 978-1-7348617-2-3
Cover design by Myrita Williams

Printed in the United States of America

www.lilettaharlem.com

ACKNOWLEDGEMENTS

I would like to thank the many people that contributed to the writing of this book!

Pamela Pine, thank you for taking time out to talk with me and provide guidance on conversations around childhood trauma, and mental health. Your work in the field is amazing! I applaud you for your many years of dedication.

Elethia Gay, thank you for sharing your story with my readers. You are an inspiration, and from the first moment we spoke I knew I wanted you to be a part of this project.

Myrita Williams, you are the best cover designer and illustrator I could have asked for. You always know how to take what is in my head and put it to imagery! I appreciate your dedication to achieving my dreams through your art!

To my Harlem family, you all support me continuously. Your love and belief in me mean so much! Thank you!

Carlos, my husband, you continue to be with me in the trenches, you help me with ideas, and your support is everything!

My mom and sister, you are two of the most important humans in this world. Everything I do reflects the love I have received from you.

Lastly, to my therapist, thank you. Thank you for making therapy a safe place. I have learned and continue to learn so much about myself. When I came to you, I truly felt lost, but you have helped me find the light out of the dark tunnel. I appreciate your professionalism and that you respect my beliefs and principles and remind me of them when I get lost. This book truly wouldn't have been possible, without the journey that I've been on with you as my therapist.

TABLE OF CONTENTS

Acknowledgements .... *iii*

Introduction 1

Part 1: Patterns And Childhood Trauma 7

Part 2: Belief Systems 21

Part 3: Perception is not reality! 31

Additional Tips for Your Journey! 38

Elethia's Story 40

Affirmations 44

Conclusion 76

THERAPY

So, they told me that I should write out my feelings and that maybe somehow, I'd feel better!

The "they" was a friend, and that I should write a letter.

Well, no, maybe it was that I should see a therapist,

well, who cares I guess!

The point is- this is my attempt at closure- at saying goodbye.

No, that's a lie.

This is my attempt at opening a door that will close all other doors.

Creating a space to address a past that wraps itself up with a pretty bow and becomes my present.

I should warn you- it won't be pleasant.

As I write these words, I ask myself,

will revelations and exposure make me better?

Well hmm…

Removing dope from an addict doesn't make them any less of a fiend.

And, airing dirty laundry doesn't make it clean.

So, I guess we shall see...

Time for therapy!

Liletta Harlem

INTRODUCTION

I was in the middle of finishing my first book, *Celebrating A Legacy*, things were going well, and as winter began to take its course, I soon started entering a depression. Now if you've read that book, you will realize that this is not new to me. In fact, me and depression, well, we go way back, old friends you might say! However, this time I began to recognize the darkness as that oh so familiar scary depression that has left me in some bad places in the past.

Other than the seasons changing, the days getting shorter and darker, I couldn't quite figure out what was causing this low. As I continued writing and reflecting, it dawned on me that this past year has been filled with changes and disappointments.

As happy as I was to be writing my first book, I had a lot going on: the pressure of changing jobs, running into financial challenges, my spiritual routine changing, becoming more active in the caregiving of my then 96 year old grandmother and also caring for my mom who had a major back injury, and was experiencing other health issues, and lets just add, still being a relatively new wife, who occasionally suffers from PTSD from a previous abusive relationship! Oh, and my father passed away without me getting a chance to say goodbye. Let's not forget about the concussion from bumping my head either! Yeah! Thinking about it in that way, I guess I could begin to understand why the dark cloud was beginning to settle on my life.

As the book was getting closer to completion, I was getting deeper into depression. Having battled this foe before, I've put things in place to ensure that I don't get to those places that have me back in the hospital and on suicide watch, which I talk about in my previous book. So, as I got emotionally darker and darker, I started doing the mental checklist to see where I was and if I needed help. It soon became apparent that I was going to have to tap into some additional resources to get myself back on track and where I needed to be mentally.

I started talking with a good friend and she suggested therapy, something I am remarkably familiar with. While it was successful in prior years, I was proud of being past the therapy days. It had been years since I had used therapy and medication, and it felt like a step backward to even be considering these options. Fortunately, I did not let that keep me from getting the help I needed. I talked to my doctor and I found a therapist.

This book is designed to share a bit of that journey of my therapy and self-discovery. With my first book, I wanted to get the conversations started. But, sometimes, when those conversations start, you might be stuck with, okay, so now what? How do I go from conversations to healing?

I am going to share some of the lessons I've learned, am learning, and this will also be used in the various workshops and events that I am conducting around this topic. This book is based on my years of researching, therapy, and taking several psychology classes. *Throughout this book I will consistently highlight that nothing I have written is designed to treat, diagnose or replace professional medical assistance.* This is simply me sharing my journey of what I have learned, and what has helped me and many other women that I have shared these experiences with.

Lastly, someone once asked me, "If you still battle with depression, still have moments of self-doubt, why do you feel you should help other people if *you aren't there yet?*" My answer is this. I represent the strong woman that recognizes she is not invincible. I speak to the women who, like me, get up every day talk through the self-doubt, put their capes on, and remain a superhero for the world. I reflect women who experienced trauma from their past, but who refuse to stay stuck! Ladies, if I can do it, you can do it. Whatever is broken, damaged or needs correcting, we have within us the strength, power, and courage to fix it.

I can fix my....

CHASING THE

Chasing the high.
Chasing the low.
Not wanting to crash.
But how low can I go?
Reckless endanger,
Buried down anger.
Which poison will kill me?
I never know.
I sell my body.
But I never gain.
There's not enough substance,
To cover the pain.
I live for tomorrow.
I cannot face the day.
The voices convince me
I'm in my own way.
I dance for the people.
The laughs are for free.
A standing ovation.
For the actor, not me.
How long can I go?
Not wanting to crash.

I CAN FIX MY...

Chasing the low,
Chasing the high,
If I should wake,
Before I die,
Chasing the low.
Chasing the high.
Liletta Harlem

PART 1

PATTERNS AND CHILDHOOD TRAUMA

We all have probably met a person who seems to be always waiting for the next fix, rush, or high!

In my journey it came to me that in some ways, many of us are this person.

We've chased highs and lows, learned coping techniques that have left us empty and afraid to face the hurt, pain, and tragedies we've experienced in life.

One of the first things a therapist will usually ask at the first appointment is, "Why are you here?"

And they ask this because many of us continue self-destructive paths until the need to get off that train becomes greater than the need to stay on it.

Depressive thinking, abuse, self-deprivation, addictions and any other negative behaviors, believe it or not bring us something that we translate on some level as a self-benefit. Maybe it's the familiarity of the experience, maybe it's the connection to others who may be on that same path with us, but in the depth of our consciousness we hold onto those behaviors, simply, because we want to.

The only thing that makes us change is when we no longer benefit from that train ride.

Many things can jump start or trigger the end of the track for us. It can be the reality of losing loved ones from our behavior, it may be fear, or it may be because of a financial loss from our behavior. But something must create a reason to change that is greater than the reason to stay on the negative train.

When I started back up therapy after almost 10 years of what I like to call "mental and emotional sobriety", it was because the fear of losing my most important relationships became greater than the comfort of the familiar pain of depression.

Unfortunately, even though I am currently in a healthy and happy marriage, the many years of cycling through bad choices, depression, and wrong belief systems were beginning to have their effect on me, and I knew I needed help.

DON'T SAY YOU LOVE ME

Don't say you love me.
Because those words carry the weight of every man that never did.
They reopen wounds that never healed
Giving me a false sense of security I don't need to feel

Don't join the long list of men that
Promised to never leave
Only to leave every time
Or bring me down so low
Leaving me to die

Please don't say you care
Because if you care you will know
That my emotional scars tattooed across my soul cannot be removed
Although I cover them with false confidence
Big cheeky smiles of pretense
They're there
Peaking through
So please leave me be
This is the best version you will see
The oak tree
Standing alone and powerful
Unloved
So please don't say you love me

Liletta Harlem

PATTERNS

One of the first steps that I found important in my own journey was to understand the triggers that send me into negative cycles.

To talk about this, I'm going to get a little into the brain. Now, personally, I love science, but I'm not going to make this overly scientific.

So, let me break it down this way.

You start a new job. Initially, you must plug in the directions to get to your destination. After a few times however, you find that the route is mentally automatic. So much so that on the weekend, you may automatically head toward work if you start heading in that direction. What happened?

Our brain is designed to look for patterns and connect whatever it receives to said patterns. There are many articles that will give you the scientific description of these processes. But, for the sake of this book, we are going to keep it simple.

As a child your brain begins to form connections and patterns. The person that feeds you, takes care of you immediately is associated with feelings of safety. Language, behavior, imitation, all these are various forms of your brain making connections and remembering those connections for future use. In a perfect world, you learn to love and trust the right people, and understand what a healthy fear of dangerous situations should feel like.

But what happens when there is trauma, abuse, or other negative things going on during childhood? Patterns are still formed. But these patterns may become negative coping skills, doubts, insecurities, mistrust, anger, and sadness.

In my interview with Pamela Pine, PHD, when asked about the effects of trauma when young she stated, "For one thing, the brain really isn't fully developed until the age 26 or so, so those early experiences in early childhood but also throughout youth, have a direct effect on the developing brain... how it processes information... the brain is adaptive, at the same time though when we set those patterns up early in life, those are the patterns that we tend to carry later in life, unless we have definitive intervention."

As my therapist has helped me to appreciate that one of the first steps to recognizing certain things we do is to first recognize why. To understand the relationship between how we process and how that connects to things that happened in our life that were beyond our control.

In my own journey, the relationships and feelings of abandonment from father figures in my life, and the challenges associated with growing up witnessing toxic environments, led me to form certain beliefs about myself.

Those beliefs have led me to form certain patterns and behaviors that stayed with me my entire life.

One such belief is that the men in my life will always choose someone else. Subconsciously, I believe that I'm not good enough or important enough to have a man choose to love me and not leave.

Wow! Think about the behavior that can come from that belief.

Jealousy, self-doubt, seeking validation and approval, self-sabotage are all complex emotions that could cause one to deliberately seek unavailable men. One could reason that these men are not going to stick around anyway so why not seek out the men who are not in positions to commit?

This thinking has also allowed me to get into relationships that were abusive. *When you want to hold onto a relationship so hard because you believe that the person walking away confirms your belief that you must somehow be unlovable, you will do anything to keep that relationship, you will accept any treatment as long as the end result feels like love.*

So, with that understanding, what would I do? What changes a pattern? Creating a new pattern. These were the steps I took to begin the change.

Step 1. Truth Statement: The father figures in my life that walked away, did so because of their own issues and inadequacies as adults. Their behavior was not a reflection of my value.

Step 2. Forgiveness/Releasing Power: Forgiveness is a form of acceptance; however, it does not condone behavior. Accepting that like myself, people many times stumble through life making a ton of bad choices until they finally see that those actions are hurting themselves and others. As an adult, I can accept this and forgive any adults that disappointed me.

Step 3. Self-Validation: Understanding my value. Not the value connected to the love and attention from a man. What makes me important is not the opinion of someone else. What makes me important is the value that I assign myself based on my current belief system.

Step 4. Accountability: At a certain point it becomes imperative that you take accountability for your own actions. This step isn't easy, and it can take years going through the first three steps. But eventually, you can begin to take control and have new patterns when you own your actions, and you make that separation between the child you and the adult you. The child had no ability to do anything about their circumstances. The child was truly a victim. You as an adult, have the ability and resources to change your circumstances. You can choose not to be a victim.

Now it is your turn. Try using the same formula to think about your own patterns and how you can begin changing them. *Remember, this does not replace any treatment plan your medical provider or professional has prescribed. This is an exercise to help assist with whatever your current process is.*

1. Step 1: Truth Statement: Reflect on the earliest memories of pain. Think of your age and your vulnerability. Picture someone now that is the same age that you were. Allow yourself to see the reality of your innocence. Now, face your truth. What responsibility did you have in what happened to you? How much could you change at that time? Now write your truth statement below.

2. Step 2: Forgiveness/Releasing Power: Holding onto the pain of someone's actions does not make those actions wrong. The actions were wrong on their own. Holding onto the pain will only keep you in pain. Look for ways to let go of the hold or power. This may be in a full forgiveness, or it may look different depending on the person and circumstances. Now write your forgiveness statement below:

3. Step 3: Self Validation: Assign yourself value. Try not to assign this value to external means, such as, what you do

for someone else. Try to look for inward qualities or strengths. Write your self-validation statement below:

4. Step 4: Accountability: In step 1 you wrote down essentially what you were not responsible for. Now it is time to take ownership. What behaviors are you now currently accountable for? Take time and sit with this for a moment. This can be a hard step, especially when you have been a victim in the past. But, it's super important toward changing patterns. Recognize that you are not still in a helpless position, and therefore have accountability of your actions. Now write your accountability statement on the pages that follow.

LILETTA HARLEM

I CAN FIX MY...

PART 2
BELIEF SYSTEMS

In the mid-2000s, I used to conduct a workshop for domestic violence victims. It was a 15-week course that taught women how to have healthy nonviolent relationships. One of the questions that the women would commonly ask is, "How could I end up in an abusive relationship?" They would note that they in general were smart, competent, sometimes even leaders at their jobs. So how was it, that at home, they became this powerless victim?

I helped them understand that this was because of their belief system.

To illustrate, I came up with this exercise.

I would go up to each one of them and say, "You have blue hair!" Of course, immediately, they would chuckle, assuming this was a big joke. I would then become more persistent. "You have blue hair!" Occasionally, one or two might pull out their phone camera to make sure that somehow, the light wasn't hitting their hair a certain way making it appear blue. The more I insisted, it only made me look crazy to them. After the laughter, and the curious expressions would settle down, I would ask, "At any point did you believe you had blue hair?" "NO!", they would say with enthusiasm. "Did it hurt your feelings when I said that?", "NO!", they would all say consistently.

Then I would pause, and I would say the following. "What if I came up to you and I said, "You're fat!", or "You're stupid!", or "You're ugly!", or maybe even, "You're unlovable!"? And that's when the tears would come. The ladies would almost immediately go from amused and thinking something was wrong with me, to sad, and feeling as though some great secret about them had been revealed. I would then explain, "Your abuser can gain control because they have learned what you believe you are to yourself and have used that knowledge to beat you down mentally, and gain control." Silence would enter the room. See, what we believe about ourselves is easy to confirm through external sources. That's how our brains work. The ladies were sure they didn't have blue hair, so the more I insisted, it only made me seem disassociated from reality. But when someone exploits negative beliefs we have about ourselves, it's easier to become a victim to that person if they chose to manipulate us with those beliefs.

The goal at that point was to make those negative beliefs they had about themselves just as unreal as the statement "You have blue hair!". When their abuser would go into the verbal beat downs, their homework was to mentally say, "I don't have blue hair!".

They literally would practice saying that phrase every time a negative belief crept into their minds. And it worked! Those negative beliefs lost their power, and so did their abuser. Now these women still had decisions to make regarding those unhealthy relationships, but they were on their way because they recognized a valuable lesson, we are what we believe!

But how do we get these negative beliefs anyway?

Beliefs are basically formed in two ways: by our experiences or by accepting what others tell us to be true. And, most of our core beliefs are formed when we are children.

When we have deeply rooted beliefs that we cling to subconsciously, our minds will constantly look for proof to validate and bolster them. How we think, act, and feel is based upon these beliefs.

Growing up in toxic environments, perhaps being abused or bullied in school, or other damaging events and words, can create these beliefs that we accept as truth. We believe that we aren't important, or that what the abusers or bullies said must be true. We form all these beliefs, and then enter relationships that may ultimately serve to confirm those beliefs.

So how do you change the limiting beliefs?

First step is to recognize what they are! To do this, you are going to do some self-reflecting and ask yourself some hard questions.

Are you ready?

Here we go.

Be sure to use the accompanying pages to write down additional notes!

Step 1: Get honest with yourself!

1. What areas of my life am I unhappy or lack contentment?
2. Where have I tried to make improvements but can't seem to get the results I want?
3. Where in my life do, I feel weak or powerless?

Take your time and review each question and write down your answers. Be completely honest with yourself. Now determine what belief is causing the results you have listed.

Step 2: Pick the belief you have identified and think about how it's led to negative behaviors.

For example, let us say that you realize that one belief you have is that people will leave you. Maybe this has caused you to shy away from intimate relationships. Perhaps, you do not commit to people. This could even impact your employment. You might feel that you need to leave a job right when it gets comfortable and you've developed friends at work, because deep down, that level of comfort doesn't match the belief system, so you make the negative adjustments to keep your belief true!

Step 3: Make the belief a lie! Now think of examples that prove that belief wrong. Using the previous example, "Everyone will leave me.". Think about times where people didn't leave.

Even when you felt abandoned, look to see where you were doing the leaving and not the person. Dig deep to find anything that will prove that belief to be false. Trust me, if you search hard enough the evidence will start to reveal itself.

Step 4: Replace the negative limiting belief with an empowering one. It might look like this, "I have had people in my life that did not leave". In general, people do want meaningful lifelong friendships and relationships. You add the evidence from your previous step to confirm this truth. Now you have a new belief!

Step 5: Repeat this new belief to yourself over and over! This is where affirmations can be amazingly effective! Remember, those negative, limiting beliefs were repeated for the bulk of your life. You will have to work hard to repeatedly tell yourself of the new empowering belief. But eventually it will replace it!

Now, please note, this is not an easy process. Some limiting negative beliefs will be easier to replace. Others, may take a lot more work, including getting professional help to break through. And even when you are in the habit of having empowering beliefs, those old thoughts can still creep in there. But the more you create those new roads for your brain to form patterns, the easier new beliefs and thereby new behavior becomes.

In processing my own negative belief, I was writing in my journal about a toxic relationship that I had been in and I was writing down all the negative things this person had said and done which included, lying and manipulation and then I followed with this statement, "It's okay because I enjoyed the relationship". But, because I have worked on creating new patterns, my brain immediately added two words to the statement that changed the entire dynamic of the belief. Those two words were "not" and "just". The new sentence read, "It is *not* okay, *just* because I enjoyed the relationship.". Is that not powerful? I felt empowered with just adding two words. I was not going to remove the accountability from the person simply because there were aspects of the relationship I enjoyed.

Summary: Unlike the old childhood nursery rhyme, that states, "Sticks and stones may break my bones, but words will never hurt me.". Words really do hurt. The words we tell ourselves can be extremely powerful and can either serve to continue our pain and negative behavior, or they can begin the healing process. You can't control the messages you received as a child that formed your beliefs about yourself and life, but you can begin to change those beliefs right now, with how you talk to yourself! Be sure to check out the affirmations at the end of this book. Use the space to come up with your own that are specific to your own limiting beliefs that you are replacing. Remember, you've got this!

I CAN FIX MY...

Remember, you do not have blue hair!

LILETTA HARLEM

I CAN FIX MY...

PART 3
PERCEPTION IS NOT REALITY!

Closely related to your belief system, is perception. Many people will say, perception is reality. Perception can certainly influence what you believe reality is, however, in my experience perception is only reality if we make it so.

I'll give you an example.

One of my previous coaching clients had a real struggle with how he saw himself. In certain settings, he felt confident and powerful. However, in other settings, he felt insecure and uncomfortable. He couldn't quite reconcile these two opposing perceptions. So I gave him this exercise.

"How tall are you?" To which he answered, "6 ft tall." I then asked him if he felt tall when he stands alone. To which he answered, that he did not. Next, I asked him how he feels when he stands beside someone who is 5ft tall. He then said, "I feel tall, because I'm taller than them.". "What about when you stand beside a tree, say the biggest tree you've ever seen?", I asked him. He said, that he feels small, because the tree is so huge. Lastly, I asked him did his actual height change in either of the scenarios I presented. He said, it did not.

What was the point. He was 6ft tall in all three scenarios, but his perception of himself changed based on the circumstances. But it wasn't the reality, his actual height never changed. See, many times we feel different, and our perception of ourselves changes depending on the situation we are in. But, if we can tap into the reality of what doesn't change, then we understand that's who we really are! So, his mantra was to say, "I'm 6ft tall no matter who I stand beside!" This helped him to build confidence in who he was at his core, the unchangeable reality.

How can this be applied to our healing process?

Recognize that just because you may feel some negative emotions in certain settings, that isn't the reality of who you are. When you are among certain people, based on their perceptions and experience, they may label you as one way. If someone considers you, unattractive, not smart, fat, skinny, etc., these are changeable perceptions based on their viewpoints. If you can develop who you are at your core you will recognize that doesn't change simply because of perception.

I CAN FIX MY...

Time to do some work.

Develop 3 core statements about yourself. Use the additional page to write as many positive adjectives to describe yourself as you can think of! Once finished, come back here and write 3 "I am" statements that will be your core positive reality statements.

1. I am_____.
2. I am_____.
3. I am_____.

Write as many adjectives about yourself as you can think of. Feel free to ask trusted friends and family to help you with this!

I CAN FIX MY...

I am me no matter who is beside me...

ADDITIONAL TIPS FOR YOUR JOURNEY! A HEALTHY LIFESTYLE AND AFFIRMATIONS

How do you eat an elephant? One bite at a time.

When we talk about making changes to improve our mental health, the conversation is not complete without a discussion on physical health. Often, bad habits include eating unhealthy foods, not getting enough exercise or an adequate amount of sleep. Pamela Pine mentioned earlier stated, "The brain gets its fuel from the gut, so whatever you eat directly impacts the brain."

For help on making this behavioral change, I asked a friend of mine to share her story about changing to a healthy lifestyle, and what tips she recommended to living healthy.

ELETHIA'S STORY AS TOLD BY ELETHIA GAY

Sadhguru states, "The way you eat not only decides your physical health but the very way you think, feel and experience life." Elethia, 13 years ago, would not understand this advice.

Food intimidated me well into my 30's. Food was my "frenemy". Not that I disliked food. I thought food didn't like me. It was scarce. There was never enough. When it was available, all the tasty food seemed to be bad for my health. I thought food wanted to make me fat no matter what I ate. "Good food" or "Healthy Food", was nasty on purpose. It was expensive. It was tasteless. It wanted me to go hungry. As for exercise... ha! It messed up my perm and made me feel tired. If you expected me to run after 12 years of age? I would pass!

What changed? First, to change I had to be on the stage: "Ready". I went from making excuses not to change to reasons change would save my life. According to the trans-theoretical model for change, two reasons people are in the precontemplation stage are lack of knowledge, lack consciousness of the impact of their behavior on others, or both.

When I asked my mom, a three-time cancer survivor, why she exercised and meditated she said it kept her from getting sick. It was not until the last few weeks of my pregnancy when I received my pre-cancer and pre-diabetic warning that I realized my mom had another (much deeper) reason for changing her behaviors. She wanted to be there for my sister and me. That day, as I sat in my doctor's office 8 ½ months into my pregnancy, I jumped two stages in the change model. I went from ready to change to taking action. Immediate action!

How did I change?

Whether you have a traumatic experience that causes you to change or you have experienced nothing traumatic but feel you need to change remember to start small. That is right, I am suggesting start small, not play small.

First, set a goal. I set BIG goals, so why not you? Then, I break the big goal into micro goals that include week by week daily goals. For instance, if I want to lose 30 pounds in X months, I will start with week one and a daily diet that includes: eat a chicken salad for lunch Monday-Friday and walk for 30 minutes around my neighborhood, Sunday-Tuesday at 8 am and Thursday-Friday at 1 pm.

Why micro goals? Because you do not exist in the future. You exist in the now. Deal with your body now. Take one step and then another.

Next, get an accountability partner or **partners**. Whether you hire a trainer, join an on line coaching group, or set a goal with your friend, having someone along for the ride to keep you accountable increases your odds for success. Thomas Monson said: "When performance is measured, performance improves. When performance is measured and reported, the rate of improvement accelerates."

According to The American Society of Training and Development, create follow-up appointments with an accountability partner and the odds for your success are as high as 95%.

Finally, build a relationship with your body and food. Know how your body responds to certain stimuli, including types of foods and the times you eat. Think about the first few months of dating. When you're building the relationship, you learn all there is to know about the person. Where do they come from? What are their favorite foods, snacks, movies, etc.? Why does being around them make you feel so full of life? When it's the one, you look even deeper into who they are and how you both can grow together.

If you can take that amount of time out of your life to learn that much about another person, why should learning about you be any different? What foods make you feel alive, energetic, or sluggish? What foods cause your face to break out or constipation? Learn about your body. Although many trainers suggest not weighing yourself daily, I believe at least once a week gives you a clue how your body is responding to activities that week. When you fall off track, forgive yourself and figure out what caused that misstep.

Guess what? Failure will happen more than once. Just like you forgave that cutie who broke your heart time and time again in high school, you can forgive yourself. As we mature adults realize, people make mistakes. While we don't have to suffer at the hands of an abuser because he/she is human. We can forgive and move to a higher level of consciousness, so we don't repeat past mistakes. That is what the relationship with your body and food looks and feels like.

The question you must ask yourself is, "Are you ready for a change?"

AFFIRMATIONS

Affirmations are positive self-statements. These can be beneficial in helping to change the negative words that have been repeated in your brain. Pamela Pine, mentioned earlier in this book, stated that affirmations can be helpful to give your brain a new positive path. One thing to remember, even with affirmations, your old belief systems may turn up the negative words in your head, to almost try and prove this new way of thinking wrong. Remember, the brain is designed to fight for familiar patterns. But don't give up. Keep repeating the affirmations, and then work to convince your brain that you believe it. This will mean repetition as well as actions to match. Are you ready to put in the work? At the end of my affirmations is a space for you to write down your own personal affirmations, or ones that you have come to appreciate in your own life.

You've got this!

I CAN FIX MY...

DAY 1

I can't force anyone to like me. But I can elevate myself so that their opinion does not impact me!

DAY 2

I give myself permission to say: "No!"

Day 3

My peace is priceless. I will not trade or sell it for anyone or anything. If something costs my peace, it's not worth it!

Day 4

Laugh today! Find reasons to laugh!

I CAN FIX MY...

DAY 5

I am accountable for my actions!

Day 6

I will treat my body with love and respect.
A healthy body contributes to a healthy mind.

I CAN FIX MY...

DAY 7

*I believe in myself, because,
I've won this battle before!*

DAY 8

I choose to be exactly who I am right now.

I CAN FIX MY...

DAY 9

*I will enjoy this moment.
I'm not obsessing about the next.*

DAY 10

I am focused!

I CAN FIX MY...

Day 11

I will celebrate my accomplishments. I'm not afraid to let my light shine.

Day 12

I will not take things personally.
It's rarely about me!

I CAN FIX MY...

DAY 13

I will appreciate the things I have. I will operate from a place of contentment.

DAY 14

I embrace silence. This gives me time to listen to the inner self and grow.

I CAN FIX MY...

Day 15

A person's role may be replaced but the individual experience with them is irreplaceable.

Day 16

As I work on my goals, I will still show up and show out!

I CAN FIX MY...

Day 17

I will continue to dream!

DAY 18

I will not allow anyone to take away my passion.

I CAN FIX MY...

Day 19

I will not give anyone the power to change my mood or behavior.

Day 20

I am important, but life is bigger than me. I will be modest when I get overwhelmed with myself.

DAY 21

I am going to be honest about my feelings. It's okay not to be okay. My feelings matter!

DAY 22

I will pause, reflect, relax and release.

Day 23

I am going to break the rules sometimes. I will learn from these moments and allow them to make me the best version of myself.

Day 24

*I don't have it all figured out, and that's okay.
I'm at peace even in uncertainty.*

I CAN FIX MY...

Day 25

I am not in control of anyone's behavior. I will not take responsibility for what someone else says or does.

DAY 26

I will only use positive words to describe myself.

I CAN FIX MY...

Day 27

I will look within for validation. I do not need others to give me praise in order to feel good about myself.

Day 28

I will focus on my accomplishments instead of my flaws.

I CAN FIX MY...

Day 29

I am my own success story!

Day 30

I am amazing! I am beautiful! I love me!

I CAN FIX MY...

My Personal Affirmations

For Day 31, use this page to write your own personal affirmations!

CONCLUSION
MY LOVE- THE PERFECT LOVE STORY!

You love me
Unconditionally
You look me in the eyes
Past the cries
Past the lies
And you love me

With you

I am safe
Never abused
Never confused
Because you love me

You accept the flaws
But you pause
To push me

Yes, you lovingly
Yet firmly
And ever so carefully
Convince me

I CAN FIX MY...

To keep striving
To be
The best me

Like a painting on the wall
You respect my beauty
Thanking the creator
For sculpting me.

There is not
A pain you did not feel
A wound that did not heal
A promise left unfulfilled
That you did not experience with me.

When I gave up
You fought for me.
When I sold my soul for unrequited love
You bought it back for me.

You give me the love
That all good love stories end with happily.

You adore me
You honor me
You protect me
You love me

You are me...

Many of us seek the perfect love story. There are things we desire that make us feel like we are loved. And we may spend weeks, months even years searching for those things from others.

But what if we can love ourselves enough to give ourselves the things we look for from others?

What if we can feel protected, adored, cared for, and respected from the way we treat ourselves first?

What if we can work on being a whole person? So, content with ourselves that any other person that enters is only adding too, not filling in?

The journey to find that type of self-love may take a lifetime. But the process of healing, and growth and of self-dignifying starts to pay off immediately upon starting.

Whatever is broken, crooked, slightly off can be and should be adjusted first before looking at someone else to do the fixing.

Take ownership and accountability. Change your limiting and negative belief systems. Do not rely on perception to define you. Break negative patterns. Take care of your physical health. Use affirmations to daily instill new mental patterns.

I CAN FIX MY...

By doing those things, you can be on the path to celebrating the greatest love story you can experience.

With self-love in place you too can say,

I can fix my...

www.ingramcontent.com/pod-product-compliance
Lightning Source LLC
Chambersburg PA
CBHW042329150426
43193CB00005B/60